T0193168

Blackie and Her Kittens

A True Story

⚜

by

Carol Fegley Hieronymus

Illustrated by Elizabeth Lacovara
Edited by Anthony Jason Belotto

AuthorHouse™ LLC
1663 Liberty Drive
Bloomington, IN 47403
www.authorhouse.com
Phone: 1-800-839-8640

First published by AuthorHouse 08/15/2014

ISBN: 978-1-4567-4768-8 (sc)

Library of Congress Control Number: 2011903937

Printed in the United States of America

Any people depicted in stock imagery provided by Thinkstock are models, and such images are being used for illustrative purposes only. Certain stock imagery © Thinkstock.

This book is printed on acid-free paper.

authorHOUSE®

To the memory of Frank and Bertha Fegley,
my parents Charles and Esther Fegley,
and to "all creatures great and small".

CFH

This is a true story.

$\mathbf{O}$nce upon a time, many years ago when Charles, Carol, and Richard were little children, they would often go to a very special farm in the hills of Pennsylvania. They would go with their mother and father to visit Uncle Frank and Aunt Bertha Fegley, and oh my, what a wonderful time they had on the farm!

In the summertime, Uncle Frank would wear denim overalls with no shirt, his tanned arms and hairy chest showing around the bib.

Aunt Bertha was always in the kitchen where she wore a flowered cotton bib apron over her dress.

In the kitchen was a **GREAT BIG SHINY** stove
that had a fire burning in it all the time in winter.
Coal, a black stone-like substance, burned with
a great heat that baked delicious pies made
from apples that grew on trees out back.

The kitchen always smelled delicious from the yummy food cooking in the oven. Out from the back door, behind the kitchen, was another room, a summer kitchen, with another stove which was used in the summertime keeping the heat out of the house.

Uncle Frank and Aunt Bertha did not have a bathroom in the house so they took their baths in a big tub in the summer kitchen.

Instead of a toilet, at night they used a chamber pot with a lid. The pot had pine oil in it to make it more pleasant. In the morning, the pot was dumped down a hole in the privy which was a little house up the path behind the farm house. It had a crescent moon carved in the door. The privy had a seat with a hole in it. During the day, everyone would use the privy instead of the chamber pot. On rainy days they ran quickly up the path to keep from getting wet.

Charles, Carol, and Richard loved to go to the farm in Quakake. They loved to visit Uncle Frank and Aunt Bertha. There was so much to see and do and so many good things to eat.

In the old barn, were many old rusty farm tools, a tractor, lots of hay to jump in, some chickens who roamed around, and many barn cats to keep the mice away. A cow mooed softly to her calf in a stall. The barn was dark but light peaked in between the loose boards. The smell of fresh hay greeted the children when they went inside where they could jump and play in the hay.

Up on a hill, in a wooded area behind the house was a pig pen with a few pigs and one big, fat mother pig who had eleven new baby pigs. Mother pig was so good to her little ones. She was happily lying on her side as they scrambled to drink the rich milk from her teats.

Hanging on the fence that surrounded the pen, the children laughed and laughed at the eleven piglets clambering all over each other, squealing and pushing and shoving to get at the "milk bar."

When the mother pig stood up to walk around the pen, Uncle Frank exclaimed, "NOW THAT'S A REAL SOW BELLY!" Her belly was so full of milk and stretched that it dragged along the ground.

Across the road from the farmhouse was a large field where Uncle Frank and Aunt Bertha raised corn, tomatoes, squash, cucumbers, string beans, peas, and other delicious vegetables. Beyond the vegetable field were acres and acres of hay and corn growing to sell to other farmers for food for the cows.

Quakake was a wonderful place to visit.

One summer, a very special event happened on the farm. Uncle Frank had a sweet, playful female dog named Blackie. She was a good dog, a lively dog, and a very smart dog. When Uncle Frank would throw something he would shout, "Get that bum!" and Blackie would run, get it, and bring it back to him. She would do it over and over again and never seem to get tired.

But Blackie was not happy. Everywhere she looked around the farm, the other animals were having babies of their own.

The chickens had their baby chicks,

the ducks had their ducklings,

and the cows had their calves,

the pigs had their piglets, and the cats had their kittens. But poor Blackie, she had no puppies of her own and she was very sad.

One day, Blackie followed Uncle Frank into the barn and she saw a mother cat nursing four very little kittens. The cat didn't notice Blackie looking at them but kept on with her work nursing and licking her babies' faces.

Blackie had an idea. She decided that she would adopt the kittens for her own. They were cute, and they were little, and she must have thought the mother cat wouldn't care or else she didn't even worry about it. Blackie didn't know the meaning of the word kidnapping or kitnapping. All she knew was that she wanted babies of her own.

One day when the mother cat was warming herself and napping on the sunny side of the barn, Blackie sneaked in where the kittens were sleeping together and one by one she took them gently in her mouth and carried them to the basket Aunt Bertha had left sitting on the back porch.

When the mother cat discovered her babies were missing, she took off to search for them to bring them back to the barn. When she finally found them, there they were in the basket, all cuddled up with Blackie.

One bark from the kitnapper told the cat that she had better back off. She must have felt very angry and worried about how her babies were going to get fed.

The children's father saw the kittens in the basket with Blackie so he went to get his camera. When he came back, much to his great surprise, he saw the kittens nursing from Blackie. Everyone else, Uncle Frank, Aunt Bertha, Mother, Charles, Carol, and Richard, came to look. When their father gently lifted one of the kittens away from Blackie, lo and behold, there was a drop of milk. Blackie the dog who had never had puppies was nursing her adopted kittens. It seemed to be a miracle.

Now Uncle Frank was a big tease and one day while the children were still visiting the farm, he took each of the kittens out of the basket and hid them from Blackie. He hid one in the privy.

He hid one under the front porch.

He hid one under the back porch.

He hid one in the kitchen.

Then he waited.

When Blackie came back to the basket to be with her babies, she saw that they were all gone. She went wild with worry and began to whine, and bark, and cry, and run here and there.

It made the children feel sad to see Blackie so upset, but Uncle Frank knew that his dog was smart and as they all watched and waited, Blackie ran to the privy, picked up the first kitten gently in her mouth and brought it back to the basket. Then sniffing and searching, Blackie found another under the front porch, the third under the back porch, and finally, she found the fourth one in the kitchen in the woodbin by the stove. And one by one she brought them back to the basket on the porch. Blackie got in with her babies and they all settled down happily.

Everyone supposed that the mother cat got used to the idea that her babies had a new mom. She contented herself with grooming her fur and sleeping in the sun when she wasn't chasing the mice in the barn.

That all happened a long time ago. The children have grown up and their father, mother, Uncle Frank, and Aunt Bertha have all gone to heaven. Blackie and her kittens have gone too, but no doubt the descendents of the kittens still live on at the wonderful farm in Quakake, Pennsylvania.

THE END

Printed in the United States
by Baker & Taylor Publisher Services